Priscilla Hauser's BOOK OF FRUITS & BERRIES

NORTH LIGHT BOOKS
CINCINNATI, OHIO
www.nlbooks.com

DEDICATION

This book is dedicated to Tiny, our adopted 11-lb American Eskimo dog. She was badly abused in a puppy mill and is blind in one eye. My prayer is for people to adopt, neuter and financially support the fine organizations that work to save our animals. A portion of my royalties will go to these organizations.

ACKNOWLEDGMENTS

I wish to thank all the people who made this book possible. I wish to especially thank Heather Dakota, my editor, and Christine Polomsky, my photographer, at North Light Books. An extra special thanks goes to Joyce Beebe, Alta Bradberry, Connie Deen, Judy Kimball and Naomi Meeks who are the painters that help me prepare surfaces, paint with me and stand by me through it all. I also wish to thank the people at Plaid, Loew-Cornell, Masterson Art Products and Walnut Hollow for their support of decorative painting and their continuing efforts to create excellent products.

Other fine North Light Books are available from your local bookstore, art supply store or direct from the publisher.

05 04 03 02 01   5 4 3 2 1

Library of Congress Cataloging-in-Publication Data
  Priscilla Hauser's Book of Fruits & Berries. – 1st ed.
p. cm.
Includes index.
ISBN 1-58180-084-3 (alk.paper)—ISBN 1-58180-070-3 (pbk : alk paper)
1. Painting—Technique. 2. Fruit in art. I. Title: Book of Fruits & berries. II. Title
TT385 .H37 2001
745.7'23—dc21   00-048671
                                   CIP

Editor: Heather Dakota
Cover Designer: Wendy Dunning
Interior Designer: Brian Roeth
Layout Artist: Kathy Gardner
Photography: Christine Polomsky and Al Parrish
Production Coordinator: Emily Gross

ABOUT THE AUTHOR

Priscilla Hauser leans back in a chair, smiles and says her life is and continues to be a celebration. This remarkable, energetic blonde has been teaching decorative painting for more than 40 years and writing books for more than 30. Priscilla lives with her husband Jerry in Tulsa, Oklahoma. Their children are now married and Priscilla has three grandchildren. In addition, two adopted American Eskimo dogs are an important part of their world. Besides painting and teaching in her beautiful studio by the sea, located in the Florida Panhandle, Priscilla enjoys fund-raising for her favorite charities, which are organizations that aid animals. You can often see Priscilla on Home & Garden Television's *Carol Duvall Show*, gleefully trying to teach Carol to paint, or laughing with Susan Powell on the Discovery Channel's *Home Matters*. Priscilla has hosted a number of her own public television shows and has traveled the world teaching the joy of painting to thousands. You can chat with Priscilla and find fabulous how-to decorative painting and home decor projects online at IdeaForest.com. For a seminar brochure and other information, visit Priscilla at her Website priscillahauser.com or write to her at P.O. Box 521013, Tulsa, OK 74152-1013.

table of Contents

INTRODUCTION

I've always loved to paint with oils. Blending fruits in a rainbow of colors is so easy to do. I find oils to be very user friendly, but it has long been my wish to develop a line of acrylic paints and mediums that would enable acrylics to blend as smoothly as oils. With the help of an excellent chemist at Plaid Enterprises, it has become a reality. FolkArt Artists' Pigments and FolkArt Blending Gel Medium are incredible to work with and I hope you'll give them a try. This combination will enable you to paint fruits and berries with the elegant look of oils. I beg you to read the instructions carefully and practice, practice, practice on raw, unsealed wood. Following the instructions in this book you'll be able to paint exquisite fruits and berries. Happy painting!

Priscilla Hauser

Projects

HOLLY & BERRY SLEIGH

LEMON PLATE

STRAWBERRY WHEELBARROW

BOWL OF PEARS

PLUMS ON A TIN CANISTER

BLACKBERRY CANDLE & HOLDER

LITTLE ROCKER COVERED WITH FRUIT

FRUIT GARLAND ON FAUX TILE TABLE

A TISKET, A TASKET, APPLES ON A BASKET

Chapter One

Supplies

GENERAL SUPPLIES

These are the supplies I use when I paint:

- Pencil
- Masking tape
- Soft, absorbent 100% cotton towels or rags
- Wet towelettes
- Dry or utility palette
- Scotch Magic Tape
- Styrofoam plates
- Plastic wrap
- Palette knife
- Petit fours (small, square sponges) for basecoating and creating stripes and borders
- Plaid Stencil Decor Daubers
- Foam brushes
- Masterson Sta-Wet Palette
- Tracing paper and stylus for transferring patterns
- Black and white graphite paper
- White chalk pencil
- Cheesecloth for applying stain
- Brown paper bag for very light sanding
- Paper towels
- Brush basin
- Brush cleaner
- Toothbrush for spattering
- Clear acrylic spray, matte

Some people may prefer to use a dry or wax-coated palette for acrylics. In most cases I prefer to use the Masterson Sta-Wet Palette to keep my paints from drying too quickly. The Masterson palette consists of a plastic tray that holds a wet sponge. The special paper that is included should be soaked in water for 24 hours, then placed on the wet sponge. Blot the paper with a soft, absorbent rag to remove excess water. When your acrylics are placed on the properly prepared palette they will stay moist for a long period of time.

PAINT

FolkArt Artists' Pigments are superior-quality fine artists' acrylics in squeeze bottles. Because Artists' Pigments are of a thicker consistency, the opening on the lid is larger than most acrylic paints.

Regular FolkArt Acrylics are more like paint for your walls. The quality is excellent and I use them often for basecoating, undercoating and occasionally for the project itself.

FolkArt Metallics are wonderful. These beautiful metallic colors enable an artist to create unique special effects.

Artists' Pigments have a different chemical formulation and are slower to dry and cure than the regular FolkArt Acrylics. This is why I often undercoat with the FolkArt Acrylics and then use the Artists' Pigments for the decorative painting.

BRUSHES

Please invest in the best brushes you can afford. You'll need synthetic brushes for acrylic painting. My favorite brushes are Loew-Cornell Golden Taklon series 7300 flats; series 7200 rounds, and series 7500 filberts.

The size of the brush you choose will depend upon the size of the area you are painting. Small designs require small brushes. Large designs require large brushes. Using the proper type of brush is essential for decorative painting.

Flat brushes are used for stroke-work and for blending color. Round brushes are traditional stroke brushes. Liner brushes are used for lines and details. Mop brushes are used for finishing touches and smoothing when blending.

CARING FOR YOUR BRUSHES

After you finish painting for the day, wash the brush in brush cleaner being careful not to damage the hairs.

Work the brush back and forth in the cleaner to remove all the paint and pigment from the brush. Wipe it on a soft, absorbent paper towel.

Leave the cleaner in the brush and shape the brush with your fingers. Next time you want to use the brush, rinse it in water.

MEDIUMS, SEALERS & VARNISHES

FolkArt Glazing Medium: This medium is mixed with paint to make the paint more transparent. You can create stains, glazes that go over other colors, and many faux finishes.

FolkArt Floating Medium: This medium simplifies the floating technique. It is easier to float a color with paint and floating medium than with paint and water. The floating medium is thicker than water and does not allow the paint to travel completely across the brush, giving you a nice gradation of color.

FolkArt Blending Gel Medium: This medium makes blending acrylics much easier by keeping your paints moist and giving you more time to blend colors together.

Glass & Tile Painting Medium: This medium gives tooth to a non-porous surface, increasing the durability of the paint on glass, tile and tin.

Crackle Medium and Eggshell Crackle: The crackle medium produces large cracks and the eggshell crackle produces fine, cracked-porcelain like cracks.

To prepare your surface for painting you'll need:

- Sandpaper or a sanding disc in several grits
- Wood filler for nail holes and rough areas
- Rubber gloves (optional)
- Tack rag for wiping dust

You may also want to use a sealer. See page 11 for a detailed explanation.

Water-based varnishes will finish and protect your project. All are brushed on and dry quickly. They are available in matte, satin and gloss finishes.

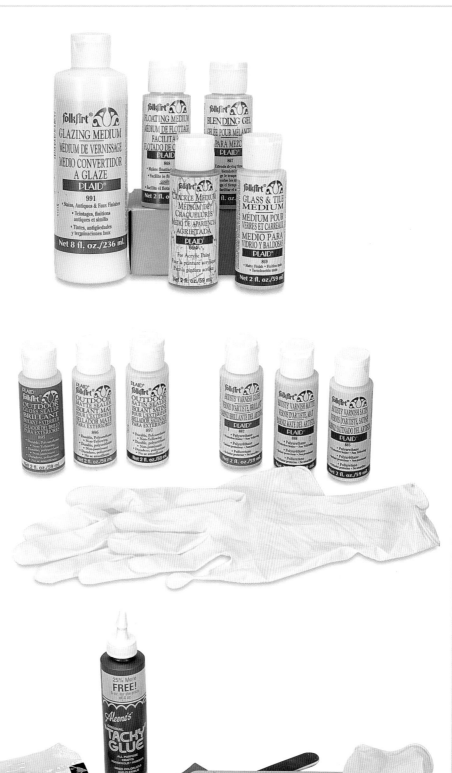

Chapter Two
Skills

YOUR PALETTE

To prepare your Sta-Wet Palette, add water plus two drops of ammonia to stop mold and mildew. The water must come to the top of the sponge. Soak the paper in water for twenty-four hours or put it in the microwave for five minutes. Before using, wipe the excess water off the paper.

CONSISTENCY OF PAINT

FolkArt Artists' Pigments are high-quality fine art acrylics that come in squeeze bottles. Their consistency can be controlled by adding as much water or medium as needed.

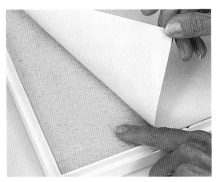

Preparing the palette.

This is the consistency of Artists' Pigment right out of the bottle.

Add a little water for a spreadable consistency like soft butter or cake icing. This is best for blending techniques.

Add more water or medium so the paint flows like cream. This is best for strokework.

Add the most water for the consistency of ink. This works best with linework.

SEALED VS. UNSEALED WOOD

Acrylics dry very fast, so it is much easier to use blending techniques on a porous, unsealed surface. When you apply blending gel medium to an unsealed surface, it penetrates and keeps the surface wet. When acrylics are applied on top of the medium, they stay wet and blend longer. If you are working on a sealed surface the blending gel will dry much faster. When you are first learning to blend with acrylics, practice on an unsealed surface. Finishing the surface with varnish will be sufficient to seal it.

As you can see here, the wood is divided into four sections. The top left is raw wood, unsealed. The top right is sealed with a coat of acrylic. The lower left is stained and sealed with wood sealer. The lower right has been stained but not sealed. You can tell that the top left and the lower right will be easier to blend on by the way the water beads up rather than soaking in.

FLOATING COLOR

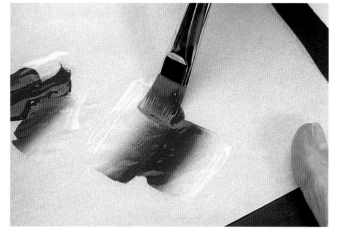

1 Squeeze a small amount of floating medium on a dry palette. Dip one corner of the brush into the floating medium and the other corner into color. On a matte surface, like tracing paper, blend on one side of the brush. Then, flip the brush and blend on the other side. Keep the brush full of paint and the paint toward the center. The paint should slowly gradate through the brush.

2 Float your color with the color facing the deepest part of the shadow or highlight.

GLAZING

After an element is completely dry, you can wash or glaze color over it. On the green apple, I glazed a transparent wash of Yellow Medium. Thin your color with water or glazing medium. Apply to the element you want to glaze. Let this dry and then apply another coat, if needed, to intensify the color.

BASECOATING

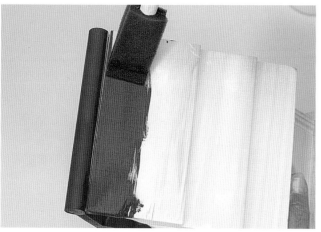

Apply color to your project (I'm painting a birdhouse here). This is basecoating. You can use a sponge brush or a 1-inch (25mm) flat brush.

UNDERCOATING VS. BASECOATING

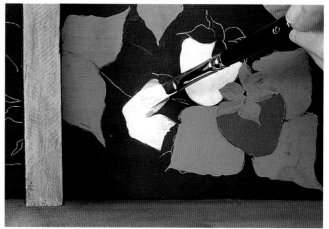

Undercoating saves you a step when basecoating. If you undercoat a design element, it will only need one basecoat. If you don't, it will need several layers of basecoat color. "Basecoat" refers to the first color on a design element. In this case the undercoat is white and the basecoat is green.

ANTIQUING

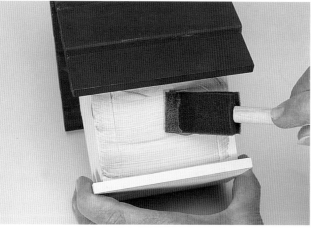

1 Basecoat the surface. (Here I've used Tapioca.) Let this dry. Make an antiquing glaze by mixing 1 part Asphaltum + 3 parts glazing medium. Apply the glaze to the surface with a sponge brush, one section at a time.

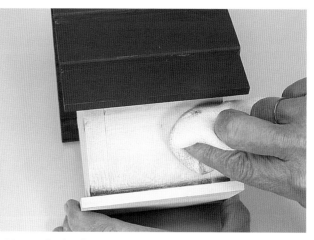

2 Use a soft, absorbent rag to wipe off the excess antiquing.

SPATTERING

To spatter or flyspeck an object, pull your thumb across the stiff bristles of a toothbrush or other spattering tool loaded with thinned paint. Flecks of paint will spatter onto your surface. Practice on a sheet of paper before you take this technique to your surface.

Double Loading the Brush

1 Stroke up against the edge of the first color of paint about forty times.

2 Turn the brush over and stroke against the edge of the second color of paint about forty times.

3 Blend on both sides of the brush with the darker color toward the center. Stroke many times to push the paint through the hairs of the brush.

4 Pick up more paint and continue blending until your brush is really full of paint.

5 If needed, pick up color on the other side of the brush and you're ready for stroking. This is a correctly double-loaded brush.

Flat Brush Strokes

1 ***Line Stroke***
Double load a flat brush with paint of a flowing consistency. Stand the brush on the flat edge.

2 ***Line Stroke***
Without putting any pressure on the brush, pull toward you, making a line.

1 ***Comma Stroke***
Touch the flat edge, apply pressure to the flat surface and begin to pull and lift.

2 ***Comma Stroke***
Gradually lift up on the flat edge with the handle pointing toward the ceiling. You can use these steps but pull to the right for a reverse comma stroke.

1 ***S-Stroke***
Stand the brush on the flat edge and begin to slide.

2 ***S-Stroke***
Let the brush fall to the left, applying gradual pressure.

3 ***S-Stroke***
Lift the brush back up on the flat edge and drag to a point. You can also reverse this for an S-stroke to the right.

Upside Down U
Stand the brush on the flat edge. Slide upward, gradually applying pressure. Lift back up on the flat of the brush.

Right Side Up U
Reverse the previous stroke for a right side up U.

Leaves

1 Apply blending gel to the leaf pattern on your surface.

2 Double load a no. 16 flat brush with Hauser Medium Green and Green Umber. Apply the shadow.

3 Pull the first stroke into the shadow.

4 Pull the second stroke so it sits in the lap of the first stroke.

5 Stand the brush on its flat edge, dark side on top, so the Green Umber side faces the tip of the leaf.

6 Pull and let it roll to the left for an incomplete S-stroke. Wipe the brush.

7 Turn your work. Double load the no. 16 flat brush with Titanium White and Hauser Medium Green.

8 Pull in the fourth stroke. Notice the placement of lights and darks.

9 Follow the contour of the leaf and pull in the fifth stroke.

Leaves, CONTINUED

10 Add the colors of your choice to the middle of the leaf. Choose the colors that coordinate with the medium value. In this case, Yellow Medium, Hauser Green Light and Titanium White.

11 Gently merge the colors together. Place half the brush on the colors in the middle and half on the outside colors.

12 Now it's time for directional blending following the growth direction of the leaf. Use a light touch. Pull from the base out. Wipe the brush, if needed. Pull lightly into the first stroke.

13 Lightly pull up into the second stroke.

14 With a light touch, make an S from the base of the leaf into the center of the third stroke.

15 Pull the fifth stroke from the base to the fourth stroke.

16 Pull from the base to the fifth stroke. Continue to follow the natural curve of the leaf.

17 Pulling back lightly from the outside edge, pull the first stroke to the base. Wipe the brush if needed.

18 Pull in from the second stroke.

19 Pull back from the tip stroke toward the base in an S pattern.

20 Pull back from the the fourth stroke toward the base.

21 Pull back from the fifth stroke.

22 Reinforce the shadow with Green Umber on a no. 16 flat brush.

23 Accent the dark edges with Ice Blue, if needed.

24 With thinned paint, paint a vein that flows with the shape of the leaf. Use the chisel edge of the flat brush or a liner brush and the leaf's darkest color.

DARK-VALUE LEAVES

Use Hauser Green Dark and Green Umber + Burnt Umber. Place Hauser Green Dark and Ice Blue in the highlight. Place Ice Blue and Hauser Green Medium in the center. Blend.

MEDIUM-VALUE LEAVES

Place Hauser Green Medium and Green Umber on the shadow side. Place Titanium White and Hauser Green Medium on the highlight side. Place Yellow Medium, Hauser Green Light and Titanium White in the center; blend as instructed.

LIGHT-VALUE LEAVES

Place Hauser Green Light and Green Umber on the dark side. Place Hauser Green Light and Titanium White on the light side. Place Titanium White and Yellow Light in the center.

HOLLY & BERRY SLEIGH

Dashing through the snow, in a *Holly and Berry Sleigh*, watch the paint brush go, floating all the way. This delightful design can be painted on many different surfaces, but what fun to paint a sleigh that can be hung on a wall, used on a table, in a bookcase or tied into a wreath at Christmas time. Or you can reduce the design and paint it on Christmas tree ornaments. What a great gift this one design could give you! Christmas is such a wonderful time of year to share your decorative painting talents, so paint a *Holly & Berry Sleigh* for your friends and family.

This pattern may be hand-traced or photocopied for personal use only. Pattern is
shown here full size.

This pattern may be hand-traced or photocopied for
personal use only. Enlarge at 200% to bring it to full
size

MATERIALS

PAINT: Plaid FolkArt Acrylics
(A) = Artists' Pigments

Licorice

Lipstick Red

Hauser Green
Dark (A)

Hauser Green
Medium (A)

Hauser Green
Light (A)

Green Umber (A)

Burnt Umber (A)

Ice Blue (A)

Warm White (A)

Titanium White
(A)

Yellow Light (A)

Medium Yellow
(A)

Red Light (A)

True Burgundy (A)

Pure Black (A)

Surface
- Wooden sleigh available from Michaels Stores, Inc., P.O. Box 619566, DFW, TX 75261-9566.
  Phone: (972) 409-1300.
  Web site: www.michaels.com.

Brushes
- 1-inch (25mm) foam brush
- ¾-inch (19mm) wash brush
- Nos. 0, 6, 8, 10 and 16 flats
- No. 1 liner

Additional Supplies
- General supplies from page 6
- Plaid Stencil Decor Dauber
- FolkArt Glazing Medium
- FolkArt Crackle Medium
- FolkArt Floating Medium
- Clear acrylic spray, matte

Prepare the Oval

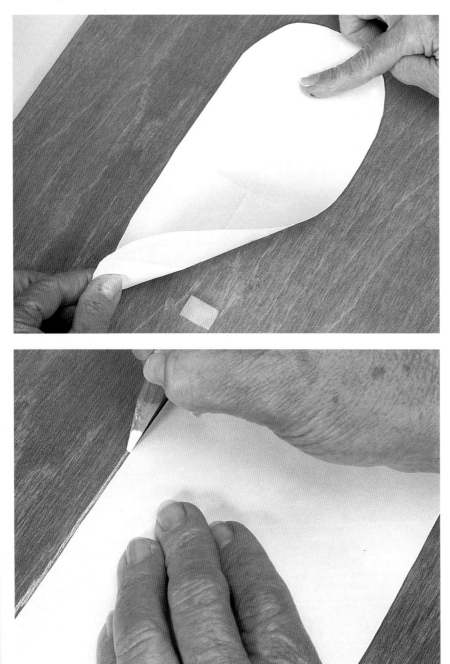

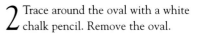

1 Stain the surface as instructed in the Strawberry Wheelbarrow project on pages 46-47. Cut an oval the size shown on page 20. Using double-stick or rolled tape, adhere the oval to the surface.

2 Trace around the oval with a white chalk pencil. Remove the oval.

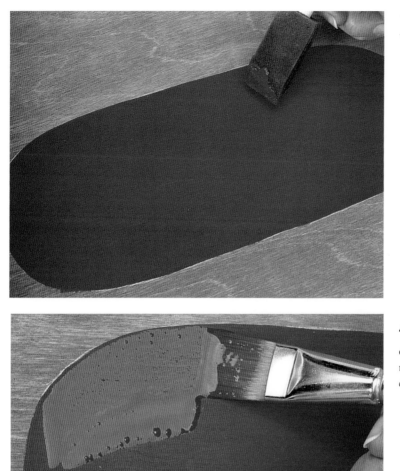

3 Apply Lipstick Red to the oval area using a 1-inch (25mm) foam brush.

4 Following the manufacturer's directions, apply the crackle medium on the red oval area very generously using a ¾-inch (19mm) wash brush. This method will give you large crackles. Let this dry as directed on the bottle.

5 Using a 1-inch (25mm) foam brush loaded with a lot of Licorice, brush over the red oval and crackle medium. The cracks should start to show almost immediately. Let this dry. When dry, mist the surface with several light coats of matte clear acrylic spray.

Holly, Pine Sprigs & Mistletoe

1 Undercoat the leaves with Hauser Green Dark, Hauser Green Medium and Hauser Green Light as shown here. Undercoat the mistletoe berries with Wicker White and the holly berries with Lipstick Red.

2 Paint the pine sprigs with a no. 1 liner brush loaded with thinned Hauser Green Dark, Hauser Green Medium, Hauser Green Light and Ice Blue, consecutively.

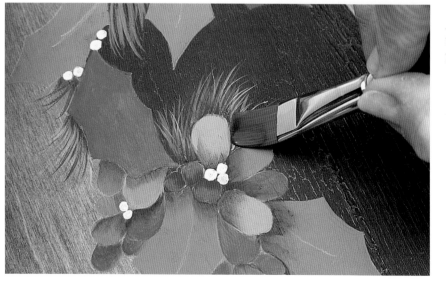

3 Shade the pine sprigs and leaves by floating around them with Green Umber double loaded on a no. 16 flat brush.

4 Double load a no. 16 flat with Ice Blue and floating medium. Float the highlight on the mistletoe leaves.

5 Load a no. 1 liner brush with thinned Ice Blue. Add the vein to the mistletoe leaves to complete them.

NOTE

You can intensify a floated shadow or highlight by letting it dry and repeating the floating process as many times as needed for your desired effect.

Holly & Mistletoe Berries

1 Double load a no. 0 flat with Green Umber and floating medium. Float the shading on the berry.

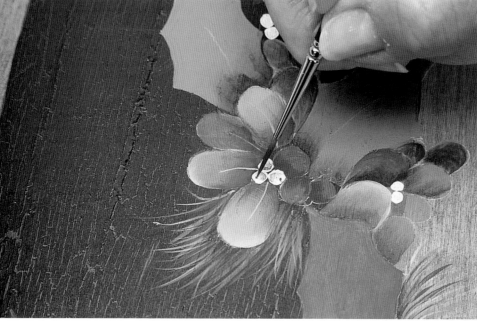

2 Add a dot of thinned Green Umber to the mistletoe berry using a no. 1 liner brush.

3 Shade the holly berries with a float of True Burgundy, loaded on a no. 8 flat brush.

4 Using a no. 8 flat brush double loaded with Ice Blue and floating medium, highlight the holly berries.

5 Add a thinned Titanium White highlight dot with a no. 1 liner brush.

Fun & Easy Holly Berries

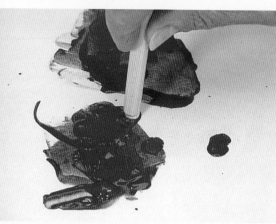

1 Load a dauber with Lipstick Red.

2 Blot and roll the edges of the dauber on a paper towel.

3 Press the dauber straight down on the surface to create a round holly berry.

4 Apply the shadow using the dauber side loaded with True Burgundy. Don't forget to blot it on a paper towel first.

5 Apply the highlight dot using a no. 1 liner brush loaded with thinned Titanium White.

The Holly Leaves

1 Create a highlight on the holly leaves by applying a float of Ice Blue using a no. 16 flat brush.

2 Use the same brush to create the vein down the middle of the holly leaf.

3 Using a no. 16 flat brush and Green Umber, shade the vein on the opposite side of the highlight.

4 Pull Green Umber from the center vein out to the edge of the leaf, following the contour. Use a no. 16 flat brush.

The Final Details

1 With a no. 16 flat brush double loaded with Hauser Green Light, float a little contrast near the base of the leaf by the center vein.

2 With a no. 1 liner brush loaded with thinned Ice Blue, add curlicues randomly to the design.

The Completed Sleigh

Holly & Berry Sleigh

LEMON PLATE

As a child, I always loved eating lemons and drinking lemonade. The miracle of picking a lemon from the tree and eating it fresh is a wonderful experience. Just think of all the things you can make with lemons—lemonade, lemon meringue pie and lemon chiffon.

You can have as much fun painting these lemons. They will look great on a wooden plate or bowl. You could also put them on a clock, or how about a kitchen stool? Remember, whether you are eating them or painting them, enjoy these little drops of sunshine.

This pattern may be hand-traced or photocopied for
personal use only. Pattern is shown here full size.

MATERIALS

PAINT: Plaid FolkArt Acrylics
(A) = Artists' Pigments

Licorice

Hauser Green
Dark (A)

Hauser Green
Medium (A)

Hauser Green
Light (A)

Green Umber (A)

Burnt Umber (A)

Ice Blue (A)

Titanium White
(A)

Warm White (A)

Yellow Light (A)

Medium Yellow
(A)

Raw Sienna (A)

Burnt Sienna (A)

Asphaltum (A)

Yellow Citron (A)

Surface
• Walnut Hollow 11½-inch (29cm) round, wooden plate, no. 3526

Brushes
• 1-inch (25mm) foam brush
• ¾-inch (19mm) wash brush
• Nos. 6, 8, 10, 12 and 16 flats
• No. 1 liner

Additional Supplies
• General supplies from page 6
• FolkArt Glazing Medium
• FolkArt Eggshell Crackle
• FolkArt Floating Medium
• FolkArt Blending Gel Medium

Prepare the Surface

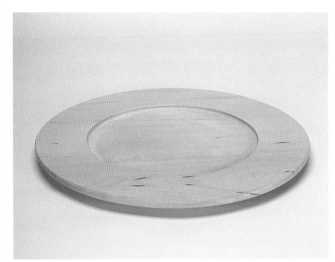

1 Here's how the unfinished wooden plate looks before painting.

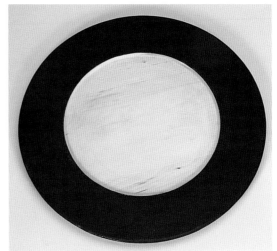

2 Basecoat the rim of the plate with Licorice.

3 Very lightly stain inside the black rim of the plate with a mix of 4 parts glazing medium + 1 part Asphaltum using a 1-inch (25mm) sponge brush. While the stain is still wet, double load a ¾-inch (19mm) wash brush with glazing medium and Asphaltum. Blend on a piece of tracing paper to gradate the color in the brush from dark to clear.

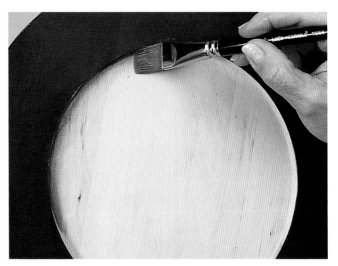

4 Float the Asphaltum around the inner edge of the plate using the ¾-inch (19mm) wash brush and let dry. Rub with a piece of brown paper bag to smooth the nap of the wood. Neatly trace and transfer the pattern.

Paint the Lemon

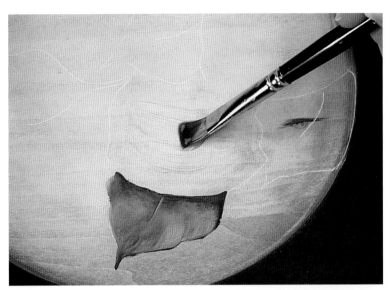

1 Paint the underneath leaves according to the directions on pages 15-17. Apply blending gel to the lower lemon.

2 Using a no. 16 flat brush double loaded with Burnt Sienna and blending gel, anchor the shadow and the dark side of the lemon.

3 Complete the floated shadow. Let dry.

Paint the Lemon, CONTINUED

4 Add more blending gel. With the no. 10 flat brush, apply Titanium White to the center of the lemon. Wipe the brush off. Apply Yellow Light around the white center. Wipe the brush. Apply Medium Yellow around the Yellow Light oval. Double load the dirty brush with Burnt Sienna and Medium Yellow. Apply to the shadow or left side of the lemon. Wipe the brush. Double load the same brush with Medium Yellow and Yellow Citron. Apply this to the right side of the lemon.

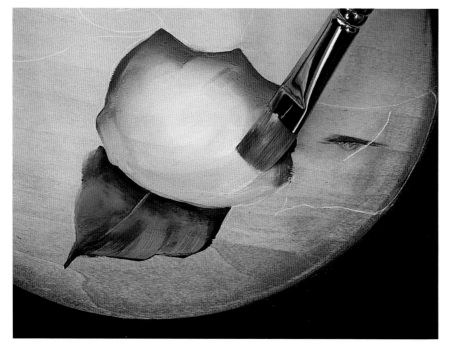

5 Blend with the contour of the lemon, but be sure to maintain the triangle.

NOTE

To create dimension it is important to paint a triangular shadow of Burnt Sienna where the ends of the lemon join the larger part. On the lemon, the dark side is gently blended in with Burnt Sienna; on the light side with Yellow Citron. Do not paint the triangle all the way across the fruit to the other side. It will look like the tip is cut off.

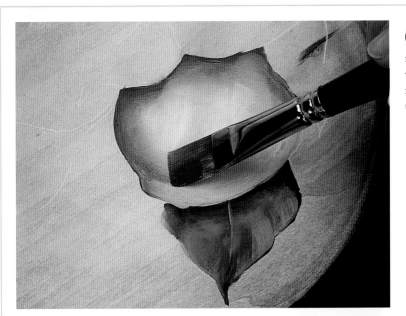

6 Move the dark into the light by cross blending. Maintain the triangle and be sure to follow the natural contour of the lemon. Use a very light touch when doing this step and don't leave the fruit spinning. Go back over it, letting the brush follow the natural curve of the lemon as in the previous step.

7 Now, paint all the leaves underneath the top lemon. See pages 15-17 for detailed instructions.

8 Paint this lemon the same as you did the underneath lemon. Follow the steps on the preceding pages. Paint the leaves on the rim.

Antiquing

1 Apply the two part eggshell crackle to the center of the plate following the manufacturer's directions. Use the 1-inch (25mm) wash brush. Let it dry thoroughly. Then, mix 3 parts glazing medium + 1 part Asphaltum + 1 part Burnt Umber, and using a 1-inch (25mm) foam brush, apply on the inside of the plate's rim.

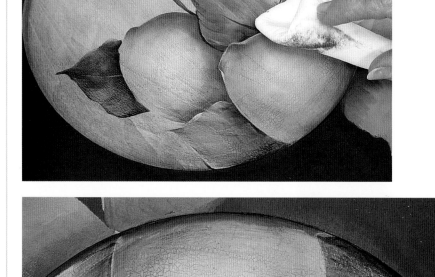

2 With a soft rag, wipe off the excess glazing medium mix.

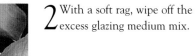

The Completed Crackle and Antiquing Process

The Completed Lemon Plate

STRAWBERRY WHEELBARROW

O ne of the wonderful things about decorative painting is that you don't have to stick to traditional colors. For example when painting strawberries, they can be a deep burgundy or a very bright red. You can add unripe berries which add beauty and originality to the design. Actually, because it's decorative you can paint them in any combination of colors you desire and that will work together with your motif.

Try these fun strawberries on many different surfaces— like boxes, cups, plates and bowls. What a great summer project! Perhaps you could paint these strawberries on a strawberry pot and give it as an exceptional housewarming gift.

This pattern may be hand-traced or photocopied for personal use only. Pattern is shown here full size.

MATERIALS

PAINT: Plaid FolkArt Acrylics
(A) = Artists' Pigments

Licorice	Lipstick Red	Wicker White	Hauser Green Dark (A)	Hauser Green Medium (A)	Hauser Green Light (A)

Burnt Umber (A)	Asphaltum (A)	Titanium White (A)	Ice Blue (A)	Pure Black (A)	Yellow Light (A)

Medium Yellow (A)	Cadmium Orange (A)	Red Light (A)	Napthol Crimson (A)	True Burgundy (A)

Surface
- Wooden wheelbarrow available from Hobby Lobby Creative Centers, 7707 SW 44th St., Oklahoma City, OK 73179

Brushes
- 1-inch (25mm) foam brush
- ¾-inch (19mm) wash brush
- Nos. 1, 2, 4, 6, 10 and 16 flats
- No. 1 liner

Additional Supplies
- General supplies from page 6
- FolkArt Glazing Medium
- FolkArt Blending Gel Medium
- FolkArt Floating Medium
- Satin varnish

Little Wooden Wheelbarrow

Prepare the Surface

1 On a dry palette mix 6 parts FolkArt Glazing Medium to 1 part Asphaltum + 1 part Burnt Umber. FolkArt Glazing Medium will not seal the wood.

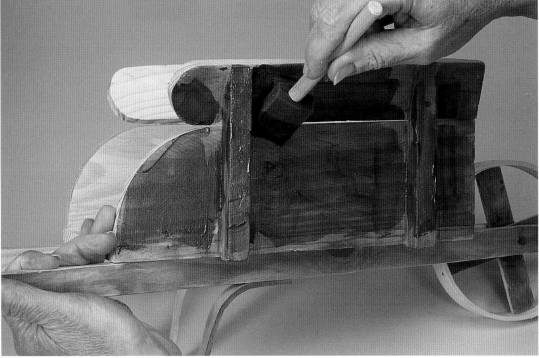

2 Brush on the stain mixture with a 1-inch (25mm) foam brush.

3 Wipe off the excess stain with a piece of cheesecloth or a soft rag. Let this dry. Rub with a piece of brown paper bag to smooth the raised grain of the wood.

4 Apply Licorice to the sides of the wheelbarrow with a 1-inch (25mm) foam brush. Let this dry. The Licorice will seal the wood making it a little more difficult to blend the colors. See explanation on page 11.

Paint the Strawberry on Unsealed Wood

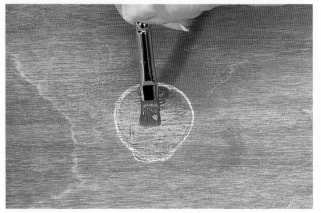

1 Apply the blending gel with a no. 6 flat brush.

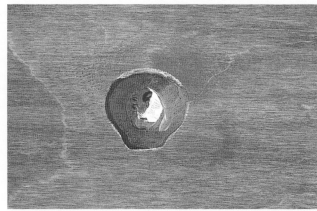

2 Apply Titanium White in the center. Apply Red Light to the right of the white, then Cadmium Orange. On the left side, apply Napthol Crimson, then True Burgundy.

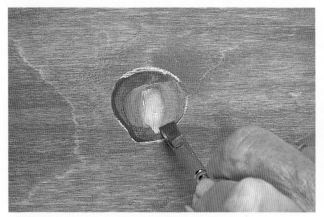

3 Blend the colors vertically following the contour of the strawberry.

4 Catch the True Burgundy and pull to the highlight side of the berry to make the berry appear round. Turn your work as needed to make painting more comfortable.

5 Pull from the highlight side to the shaded side just as you did in the previous step.

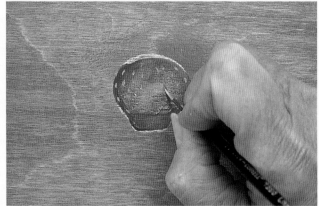

6 Apply the elongated seeds with a no. 1 liner brush loaded with thin Yellow Light. Be sure the seeds follow the contour of the berry.

7 Using a no. 1 liner or a 10/0 liner brush loaded with Pure Black thinned with water, outline the edge of each seed curving with the berry.

8 Undercoat the bracts with Hauser Green Light.

9 Using True Burgundy, float the bract shadows on the berries with a no. 8 flat brush. Apply under the bracts.

10 Float shadows on the bracts with a no. 8 flat brush loaded with a mix of Green Umber and Burnt Umber.

11 Highlight the bracts by floating on Ice Blue.

12 Paint the stem coming out of the berry with a no. 1 flat loaded with thinned Hauser Green Light. Shade the stem with the Green Umber mix. Highlight the stem with Ice Blue. The completed berry can be seen on page 51.

Sealed Surface Strawberries

1 Using a no. 6 flat brush loaded with Wicker White, undercoat all the strawberries. Let dry and cure.

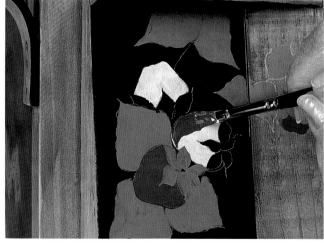

2 Undercoat the strawberries with a no. 6 flat brush loaded with Lipstick Red. Turn your work to make painting more comfortable. Let dry and cure. Undercoat the leaves with Hauser Green Medium. Let this dry.

3 Paint the leaves according to the directions on pages 15-17.

4 Using a no. 10 flat brush double loaded with True Burgundy, anchor the shadows by floating the color under the bracts and on the left side. Let this dry and cure.

5 Using a no. 6 flat brush, apply the blending gel to the strawberry you're about to paint.

6 Using a no. 6 flat brush, apply Titanium White to the center of the strawberry. Apply Red Light around that and Napthol Crimson around the Red Light. Double load the dirty brush with True Burgundy. Blend on the palette to soften and apply to the left side of the strawberry. Wipe the brush. Double load the dirty brush with Cadmium Orange. Blend on the palette to soften and apply to the right side of the berry. Wipe the brush.

7 Using the same dirty brush, blend the colors following the contours of the strawberry. Wipe the brush as needed. Use a light touch.

8 The strawberry is painted approximately the same way on both the sealed and unsealed surface. On a dark sealed surface remember to undercoat the berries with Wicker White, then with Lipstick Red. This isn't necessary on an unsealed surface.

If you don't feel comfortable...

If you don't feel comfortable painting on sealed, basecoated wood, you can come back in and paint black around the design. See an explanation of sealed and unsealed wood on page 11.

The Final Touches

Paint the curlicues around your design using a
no. 1 liner brush loaded with a mix thinned
with water of Hauser Green Light + a touch of
Burnt Umber thinned with water.

NOTE

If you are using a liner brush, the
paint you load on the brush must
be thin, thin, thin. You can thin
the paint with water or floating
medium.

The Completed Wheelbarrow
Finish the project with three coats of satin varnish.

BOWL OF PEARS

4

ears come in so many wonderful colors—yellow, green and even a beautiful red. Every time I see a pear I think of one of my favorite recipes. This was always served at four o'clock in the afternoon by Helen Hickish who owned a wonderful store called Rural Rustics. This pick-me-upper was always a welcome treat.

STUFFED PEARS

6 oz. cream cheese

2 Tbsp. brown sugar

¼ to ½ tsp. almond extract (depending on your taste)

⅓ c. toasted almond slivers

3 pears

Cream together cream cheese, brown sugar and almond extract. Add almonds, setting aside a few to sprinkle on top.

Cut the pears in half and core them to remove the seeds. Fill the hole of the cored pears with the cream cheese mixture. Sprinkle a few almonds on top and refrigerate for a few hours or overnight.

This pattern may be hand-traced or photocopied for personal use only. Pattern is shown here full size.

MATERIALS

PAINT: Plaid FolkArt Acrylics
(A) = Artists' Pigments

Licorice	Taffy	Pure Gold
Buttercup	Hauser Green Dark (A)	Hauser Green Medium (A)
Hauser Green Light (A)	Green Umber (A)	Asphaltum (A)
Titanium White (A)	Yellow Light (A)	Medium Yellow (A)
Turner's Yellow (A)	Yellow Ochre (A)	Raw Sienna (A)
Burnt Sienna (A)	Pure Orange (A)	Red Light (A)

Surface
- Wooden bowl by Wayne's Woodenware, 1913 State Rd. 150, Neenah, WI 54956

Brushes
- 1-inch (25mm) foam brush
- ¾-inch (19mm) wash brush
- Nos. 4, 6, 12, 14, 16, and 20 flats
- No. 1 liner

Additional Supplies
- General supplies from page 6
- FolkArt Crackle Medium
- FolkArt Blending Gel Medium
- FolkArt Glazing Medium
- FolkArt Floating Medium
- Water-based varnish
- Clear acrylic spray, matte

Wooden Bowl

Prepare the Surface

1 Basecoat the entire bowl with a 1-inch (25mm) foam brush loaded with Licorice. Let this dry. Paint the edge of the bowl with Pure Gold.

2 Apply the crackle medium to the inside of the bowl according to the directions on the bottle. Let dry.

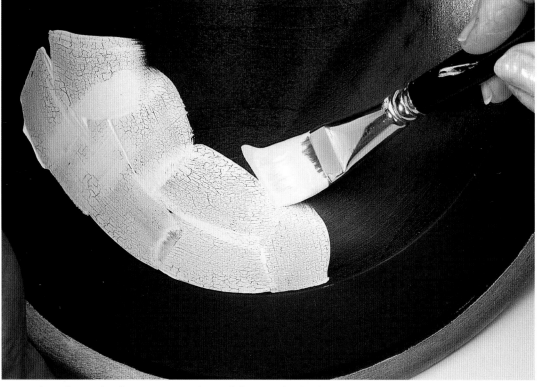

3 Apply Taffy in a flip-flop motion. Let dry. Lightly spray the dried area with several coats of matte clear acrylic spray. Let dry and cure. Neatly trace and transfer the design.

Paint the Pears

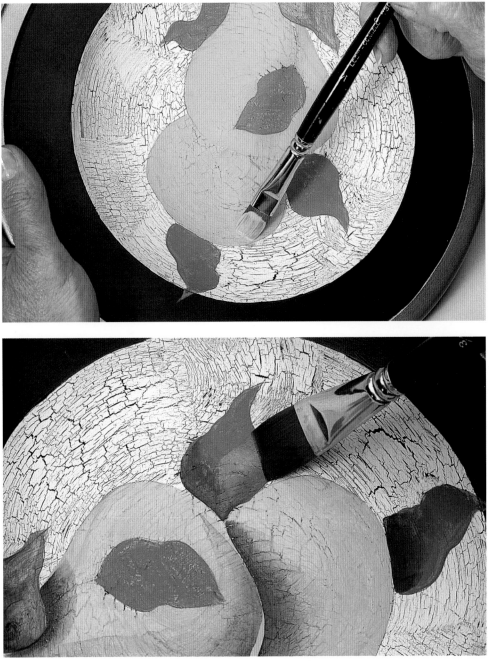

1 Undercoat the pears with Turner's Yellow and the leaves with Hauser Green Medium. Make sure your basecoat is smooth and even. You may need two or even three coats of these undercoat colors. Let dry and cure.

2 Anchor the shadows by floating on Asphaltum with a no. 16 flat brush.

Paint the Leaves

Paint all the leaves that appear
underneath the design. See pages 15-
17 for detailed instructions on painting leaves.

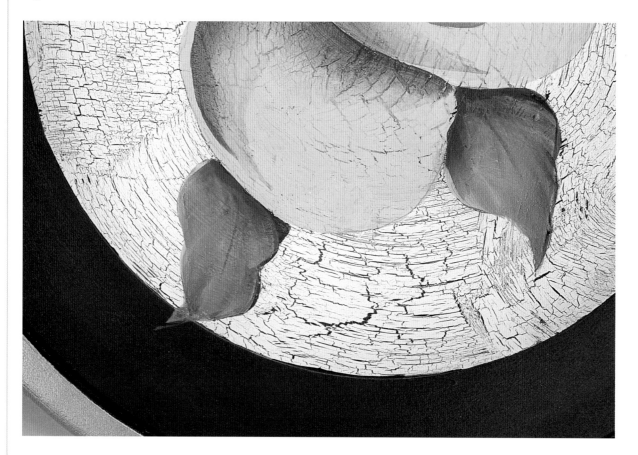

Paint the Underneath Pear

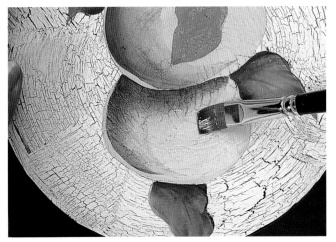

1 Apply blending gel to the bottom pear.

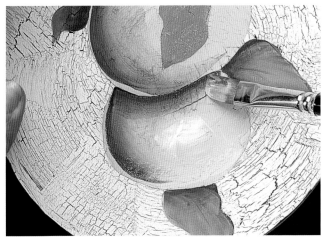

2 Using a no. 14 flat brush, apply Titanium White to the center of the bottom pear. Wipe the brush. Apply Medium Yellow around the white. Wipe the brush and apply Turner's Yellow around the Medium Yellow. Wipe the brush. Apply more Burnt Sienna to the shadow or the dark side of the pear.

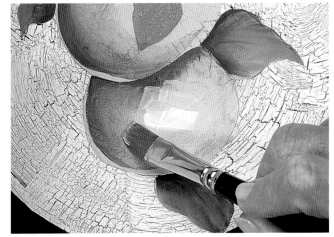

3 With the dirty brush, add a little Hauser Green Dark along the left side. Turn your work to make painting more comfortable. Wipe the brush.

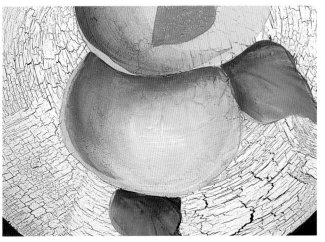

4 Quickly and lightly blend all the colors following the contours of the pear. If needed, cross blend (across the fruit), then blend following the natural curve of the pear.

Paint the Top Pear

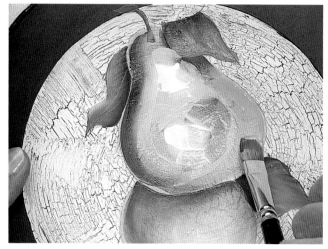

1 Paint the leaves under the top pear. Refer to pages 15-17 for more details. Apply blending gel to the top pear and add the colors just as you did on the bottom pear.

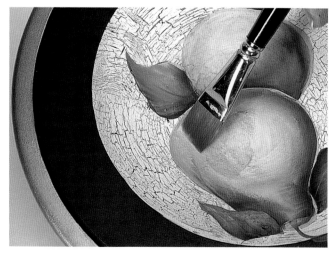

2 Blend with the natural contour of the pear. Cross blend if needed, but don't leave the pear looking as if it is spinning. be sure not to overblend. Let dry and cure.

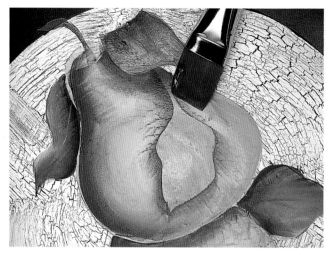

3 Float the shadow with Asphaltum around the leaf on the pear. Let dry and cure.

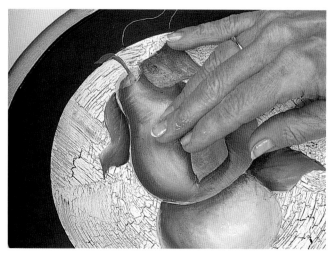

4 Wet the top pear with your finger using a little water or glazing medium.

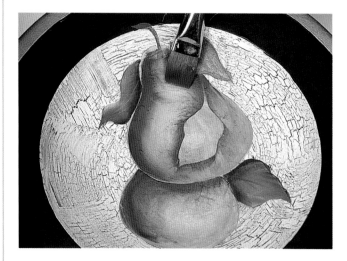

5 Apply a glaze of Burnt Sienna on the upper and lower pear using a ¾-inch (19mm) wash brush. Let dry and cure.

The Final Touches

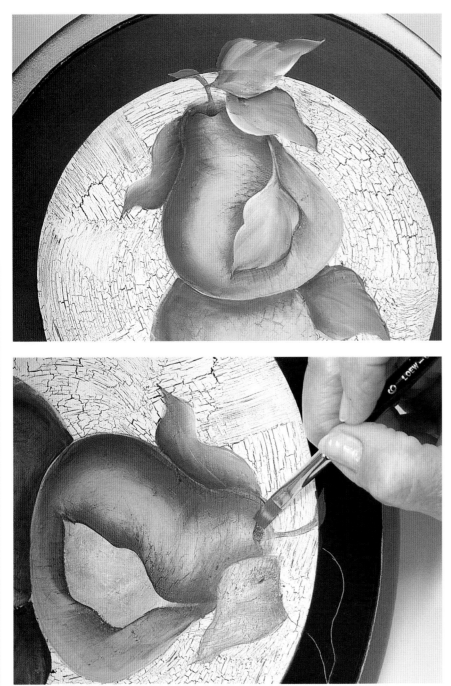

1 Float a little Burnt Sienna on the leaves and let them dry. Brush on some water or glazing medium and apply Red Light over the pear here and there.

2 With a no. 4 flat brush loaded with Asphaltum and glazing medium, make an S-stroke at the top of the pear. This will form the spot where the stem joins the pear.

The Final Touches, CONTINUED

Pear Step by Step

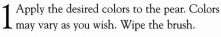

1 Apply the desired colors to the pear. Colors may vary as you wish. Wipe the brush.

2 Blend the colors following the pear's natural curve. Be sure to create the triangle shadow where the upper portion joins the lower portion of the pear.

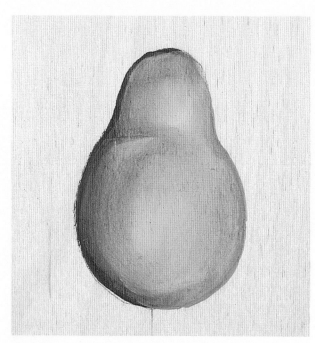

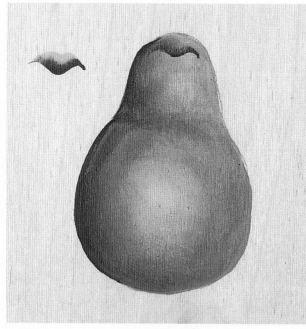

3 Add more blending gel medium and paint if needed.

4 The point of dimension is achieved by double loading the brush with glazing medium and Burnt Sienna. Glaze the pear, if you wish, with Burnt Sienna, or Red Light.

The Completed Bowl of Pears

This is one of my favorite pieces. I think it lends itself to most any decor. When the bowl is finished, dried and cured, apply two or more coats of a water-based varnish of your choice. Let the varnish dry and then rub with a piece of unprinted brown paper bag to smooth the surface. Wipe with a tack rag and apply a final coat of varnish. If desired, for a truly elegant finish apply a coat of paste wax. Turn on the elbow grease and buff to a beautiful, soft shine.

PLUMS ON A TIN CANISTER

Blues, mauves, purples and magentas! These plums were painted on a prefinished tin surface. The surface was easy to paint on. However, this is unusual, most tins are very slick. To deal with painting on a slick surface, after you have transferred your design, undercoat with FolkArt Glass & Tile Painting Medium, according to the directions on the bottle. Let this dry and cure at least ten days before proceeding. Ten days may seem like a long time, but it's a safety factor. It takes a long time for mediums and paint to dry. The paint will lift and peel if not cured, and you'll have to simply do the whole thing over. Always test your surface to see how it reacts to the products you want to use.

In this project I have applied darker colors which create a darker plum. The whimsical colors that trim this piece give a happy overall effect. However, plums can lend themselves to a far more dramatic effect—it all depends on the background choice.

This pattern may be hand-traced or photocopied for
personal use only. Pattern is shown here full size.

MATERIALS

PAINT: Plaid FolkArt Acrylics
(A) = Artists' Pigments

Gray Plum

Hauser Green
Dark (A)

Hauser Green
Medium (A)

Hauser Green
Light (A)

Burnt Umber (A)

Ice Blue (A)

Titanium White
(A)

Prussian Blue (A)

Dioxazine Purple
(A)

Pure Magenta (A)

Yellow Citron (A)

Surface
• Pre-painted tin canister available from Hobby Lobby Creative Centers, 7707 SW 44th St., Oklahoma City, OK 73179

Brushes
• Nos. 8, 12, 14 and 16 flats
• No. 1 liner
• Mop brush

Additional Supplies
• General supplies from page 6
• FolkArt Glass & Tile Painting Medium
• FolkArt Blending Gel
• FolkArt Floating Medium

Prepare the Surface

Keep your eyes open for unique pieces to paint on. I found this colorful tin canister on sale and it was pre-trimmed and ready for me to paint some plums in the center of the lid.

The Unpainted Tin

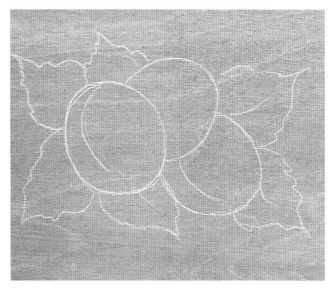

1 Chalk the backside of the design with white chalk and carefully apply the pattern to the tin or wood piece of your choice.

2 Paint the leaves as instructed on pages 15-17.

The Plums

1 Apply blending gel to the plum that is underneath the others.

2 Float an anchored shadow using a no. 12 flat brush double loaded with floating medium plus Dioxazine Purple. Let dry and cure.

3 Apply Titanium White to the center of the plum. Wipe the brush. Then, go around the white with a mixture of 4 parts White + ½ part Gray Plum + ½ part Dioxazine Purple. Wipe the brush. Apply Gray Plum + Dioxazine Purple to the left of the separation. Wipe the brush. Apply Gray Plum on the right and left sides. Add Yellow Citron across the bottom.

4 Wipe the brush then cross blend. Then blend following the contours of the plum.

5 Soften the blend and the brushstrokes using a mop brush.

6 Paint the middle plum using a no. 12 flat brush and the same colors. I used a lot of Ice Blue in this plum.

7 For the top plum apply Titanium White to the center and Dioxazine Purple around that. On the light side, apply Ice Blue. Use a mix of Prussian Blue + Dioxazine Purple for the separation. On the left edge, use Titanium White + a touch of Prussian Blue

8 Wipe the brush and blend. Then cross blend if needed. Use plenty of paint and blending gel when blending.

PLUMS STEP BY STEP

1 Apply blending gel, then the colors.

2 Using as large a brush as possible, blend with a light touch following the natural curve of the plum.

3 Continue blending. Add more gel or color as needed.

4 Complete the blending, and be careful not to overblend. You can now lightly mop away your brushstrokes.

The Completed Plums

The Final Touches

Add the squiggles and tendrils using a no. 1 liner brush loaded with a very thin mix of Hauser Green Light plus a touch of Pure Magenta. Go back over them with Titanium White. Don't try to exactly match the line.

The Completed Plum Tin Canister

BLACKBERRY CANDLE & HOLDER

6

These little blackberries are so good to to eat—tart and tangy. They are best when they have been washed by the rain, picked and eaten on the spot. Raspberries and blackberries are tiny, but no, they are not hard to paint. Using a magnifying glass helps makes it possible for you to paint the most beautiful berries in the world. And you can paint these gems in many different color combinations and on many different surfaces.

Birdhouse Pattern

Roof

These patterns may be hand-traced or photo-copied for personal use only. Enlarge at 125% to bring them up to full size.

Right Side

Candle Pattern

Left Side

Front

Candle Holder Pattern

MATERIALS

PAINT: Plaid FolkArt Acrylics
(A) = Artists' Pigments

Gray Plum (A)

Dark Plum (A)

Taffy (A)

Hauser Green Dark (A)

Hauser Green Medium (A)

Hauser Green Light (A)

Burnt Umber (A)

Titanium White (A)

Warm White (A)

Ice Blue (A)

Pure Magenta (A)

Prussian Blue (A)

Dioxazine Purple (A)

True Burgundy (A)

Raw Sienna (A)

Payne's Gray (A)

Yellow Citron (A)

Green Umber (A)

Surface
- White or ivory candle
- Wooden candleholder
- Wooden birdhouse, all from your local arts & crafts store

Brushes
- 1-inch (25mm) foam brush
- ¾-inch (19mm) wash brush
- Nos. 1, 6, 12 and 16 flats
- Nos. 1 and 2 liners

Additional Supplies
- General supplies from page 6
- Toothbrush
- FolkArt Blending Gel
- FolkArt Floating Medium
- FolkArt Clear Acrylic Spray, matte

Raw Surface—
Wooden Birdhouse

Raw Surface—Candle Holder

Prepare the Surfaces

1 Sand the wood until smooth with a sanding disk.

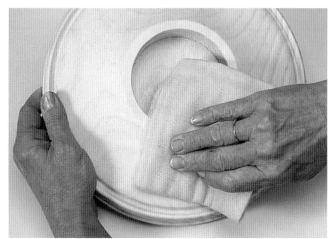

2 Wipe the surface clean with a tack rag.

3 Basecoat the surface using a foam brush loaded with Gray Plum.

4 Basecoat the trim with a ¾-inch (19mm) wash brush loaded with Dark Plum.

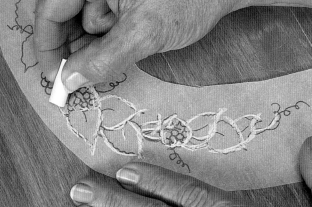

5 Chalk the backside of the traced design with white chalk.

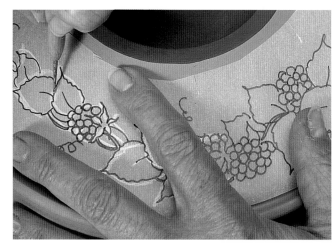

6 Carefully transfer the design with a stylus.

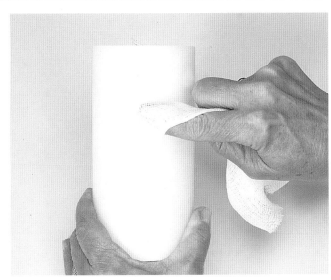

1 Rub the candle with a cheesecloth to smooth. You can also use pantyhose.

2 Spray the candle with matte clear acrylic spray to seal the surface.

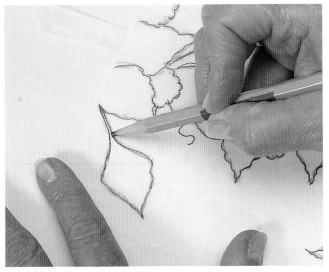

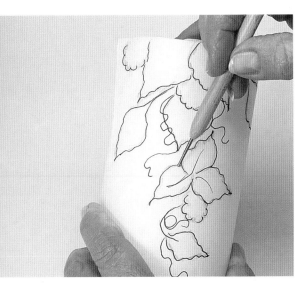

3 To transfer the pattern, go over the back of your traced design with a graphite pencil.

4 Use a stylus to transfer the design. Press very lightly, so you don't make any indentations in the candle.

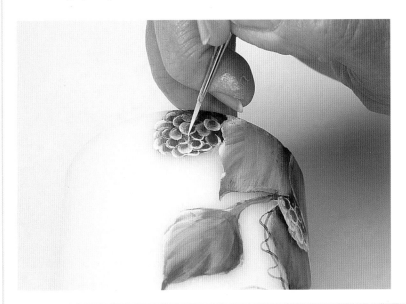

5 Paint the berries and leaves as instructed on the following pages. Let dry.

The Blackberries

1 Undercoat the leaves with Hauser Green Light and the bracts with Hauser Green Medium.

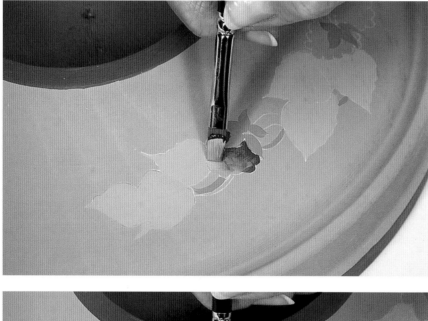

2 Undercoat the berries varying the undercoat colors as desired. Use Yellow Citron at the bottom, then Pure Magenta and Dioxazine Purple. Add a touch of Prussian Blue under the bracts.

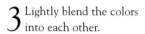

3 Lightly blend the colors into each other.

4 The berries can vary in color., using any combination of the colors listed in Step 2, page 82.

5 Float an anchor to create the shadows on the leaves and bracts with a mix of Hauser Green Dark + Green Umber. Let dry and cure.

6 Paint the leaves as instructed on pages 15-17. Use a little of the berry colors in the leaves for added interest and to unify the design.

7 Apply blending gel to the berry using a no. 1 flat brush.

8 Reapply the same colors to the berry, but with very little paint, using the no. 1 flat brush.

The Blackberries, *CONTINUED*

9 Form the berry using the no. 1 flat dirty brush double loaded with Titanium White. Make little circles around the outside edge of the berry. Then stagger the circles as they move in toward the center.

10 Make two or three full circles toward the center of the berry, picking up more white as needed.

11 Highlight the circles with a no. 1 liner brush loaded with Titanium White.

12 Clean up the edges of the berry with a liner brush loaded with Titanium White.

13 Attach the stem with Hauser Green Light. Shade the stem with Green Umber + a touch of Prussian Blue.

14 Apply a touch of blending gel to the bracts. Apply the shadows using a no. 1 flat brush double loaded with a mix of 1 part Hauser Green Dark + 1 part Green Umber.

15 Highlight the bracts with the no. 1 flat brush double loaded with the green mix and Ice Blue.

BERRIES STEP BY STEP

1 Apply Yellow Citron, Pure Magenta, Dioxazine Purple and Prussian Blue. The bracts are undercoated with Hauser Green Light.

2 Shade the bracts with a mixture of Hauser Green Dark + a touch of Prussian Blue and blend gently. Apply more blending gel.

3 Use a tiny flat brush double loaded with Titanium White to paint little circles all the way around the outside edge and staggered working in toward the center.

4 To finish, add a complete circle or two in the center area of the berry. Highlight each little section with a dot of white.

The Final Touches

1 Thin a mix of Green Umber + a touch of Pure Magenta + a touch of Prussian Blue to an inky consistency. Load this mix on a no. 1 liner brush. Make squiggles and curlicues coming out of the design.

2 Spatter the painted candle and candleholder with thinned Dioxazine Purple loaded on a toothbrush.

The Completed Birdhouse

The Completed Candle & Candleholder

Little Rocker Covered With Fruit

A beautiful needlepoint pillow covered with fruit always graced my grandmother's rocking chair. It only seemed appropriate that a garland of fruit should grace this beautiful little rocker.

Some of the fruits you've learned how to paint so far are included on this adorable rocker. However, if you can't find a little rocker like this one, try a doll's chair, a plate or a cabinet. Perhaps you can pass on a beautiful fruit memory to a young girl, just like the one my grandmother gave to me.

These patterns may be hand-traced or photocopied for
personal use only. Patterns are shown here full size.

MATERIALS

PAINT: Plaid FolkArt Acrylics
(A) = Artists' Pigments

Licorice

Pure Gold

Burnt Umber (A)

Green Umber (A)

Hauser Green
Medium (A)

Hauser Green
Light (A)

Titanium White
(A)

Warm White (A)

Yellow Light (A)

Medium Yellow
(A)

Turner's Yellow (A)

Yellow Ochre (A)

Burnt Sienna (A)

Pure Orange (A)

Red Light (A)

True Burgundy (A)

Dioxazine Purple
(A)

Prussian Blue (A)

Napthol Crimson
(A)

Surface
- Wooden doll rocker (flea market find)

Brushes
- Nos. 2, 4, 6, 8, 10, 14 and 16 flats
- Nos. 1 and 2 liners

Additional Supplies
- General supplies from page 6
- FolkArt Floating Medium
- FolkArt Glazing Medium
- FolkArt Blending Gel Medium

Prepare the Surface

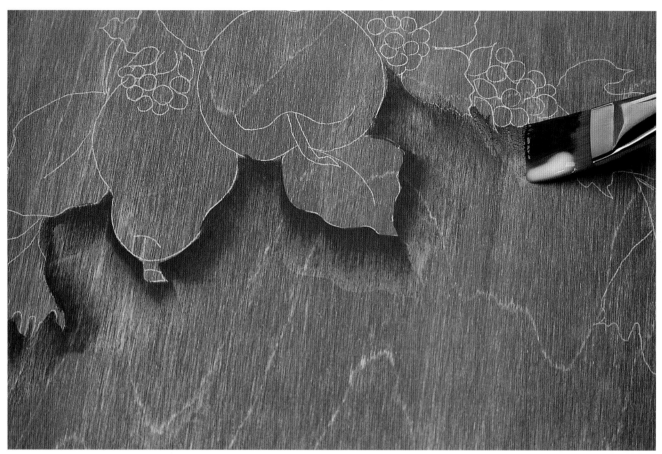

Stain the entire chair with a mix of glazing medium + Burnt Umber. Wipe off the excess with a rag and let dry. Transfer the pattern onto the chair seat. Float a shadow around the edges of the leaves and fruit with a double load of floating medium and Licorice.

The Grape Leaves

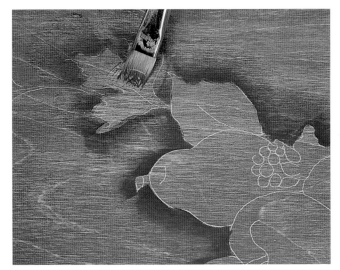

1 Apply blending gel to a grape leaf.

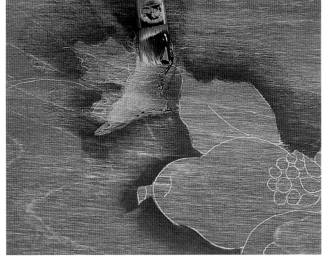

2 Anchor the shadow at the base of the leaf with Hauser Green Medium + Burnt Umber.

3 Double load a no. 6 flat brush with Hauser Green Medium and Warm White. Slowly scribble back and forth to create the jagged edge of the leaf.

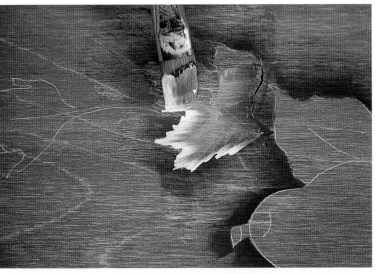

4 On the top part of the leaf apply a mix of Hauser Green Medium + Hauser Green Light. Scribble at the edge as shown. Wipe the brush.

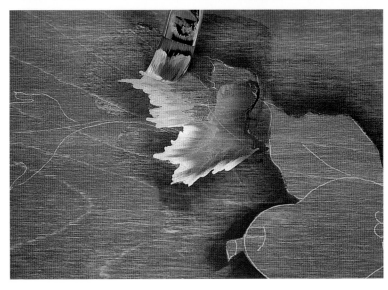

The Grape Leaves, CONTINUED

5 Apply Medium Yellow to the center, Hauser Green Light around the center, and Green Umber at the base of the leaf.

6 Merge the colors together by stroking from the base out. Wipe the brush and add more paint if needed.

7 Continue to blend by stroking from the base out to the edge of the leaf. Be sure to use a light touch.

8 Using a small mop brush, lightly stroke from the outside edges toward the base of the leaf.

9 Using a no. 1 liner brush full of thin Warm White, paint the vein. With the no. 12 flat brush, shade the vein with Green Umber. Paint all the leaves under the fruit.

The Red Apple

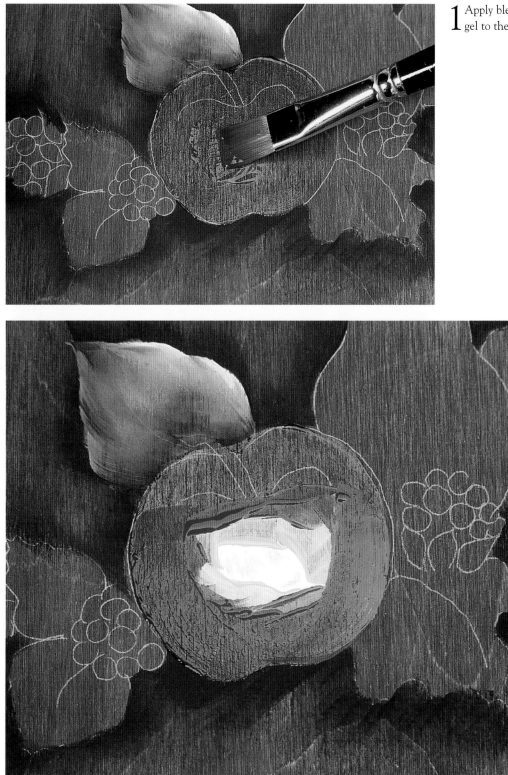

1 Apply blending gel to the apple.

2 Begin with Titanium White in the center. Apply Medium Yellow around the white, then apply Red Light around the yellow. On the right side, stroke on Pure Orange with a dirty brush. Wipe the brush and apply True Burgundy as a shade on the left side.

The Red Apple, *CONTINUED*

3 Blend downward with a no. 8 flat, following the contours of the apple.

4 Make the apple smile with Medium Yellow. Pull your strokes down from the smile to lightly blend with the other colors. Be sure to follow the natural curve of the apple.

5 Paint a "hat" on the head of the apple with Medium Yellow using a no. 4 flat brush.

6 Add Red Light and Napthol Crimson above the yellow hat. Shade on the dark side with True Burgundy and on the light side with Pure Orange.

7 Lightly pull the red down into the yellow and pull the yellow up into the red.

8 Add a True Burgundy smile in the same place you applied the yellow smile. Lightly pull the True Burgundy down around the corners.

9 Add a very tiny touch of Prussian Blue where the stem joins the apple. Lightly blend.

The Completed Apple

STEM STEP BY STEP

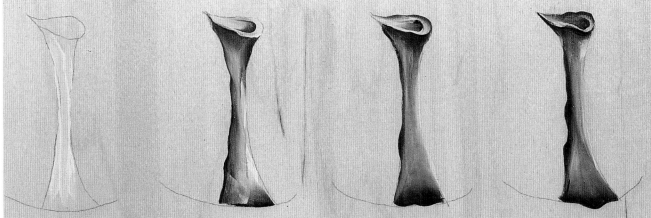

1 Apply blending gel. Then apply Titanium White.

2 Double load with Titanium White and Burnt Umber. Apply the shading and the U-stroke in the cut end.

3 Continue blending with a light touch. You may add more dark or light as needed.

4 Finish blending.

The Pear & Berries

PEAR STEP BY STEP

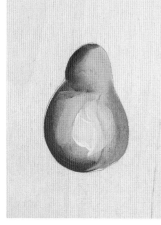  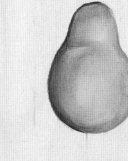 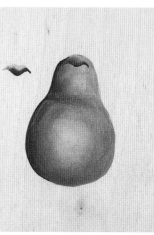

1 Apply the desired colors to the pear. Colors may vary as you wish. Wipe the brush.

2 Blend the colors following the pear's natural curve. Be sure to create the triangle shape where the upper portion joins the lower portion of the pear.

3 Add more blending gel medium and paint if needed.

4 The point of dimension is achieved by double loading the brush with glazing medium and Burnt Sienna. Glaze the pear, if you wish, with Burnt Sienna or Red Light.

BERRIES STEP BY STEP

1 Apply Yellow Citron, Pure Magenta, Dioxazine Purple and Prussian Blue. The bracts are undercoated with Hauser Green Light.

2 Shade the bracts with a mixture of Hauser Green Dark + a touch of Prussian Blue and blend gently. Apply more blending gel.

3 Use a tiny flat brush side loaded with Titanium White to paint little circles all the way around the outside edge and staggered working in toward the center.

4 To finish, add a complete circle or two in the center area of the berry, highlight each little section with a dot of white.

The Final Touches

1 Base the decorative trim on the chair with Licorice. Make little comma strokes as indicated by the pattern on page 90, using Pure Gold loaded on a no. 1 liner brush.

Detail of the Strokework on the Chair

Detail of The Rocker Seat

Priscilla Hauser's Book of Fruit & Berries

The Completed Rocker

Little Rocker Covered With Fruit

8

Fruit Garland on Faux Tile Table

Nothing adds more personality and warmth to a room than a piece of hand-painted furniture. This wonderful table with its faux tile and painted fruit is terrific. Take your time and you'll do a great job. And you'll have fun creating it.

This pattern may be hand-traced or photocopied for personal use only. Enlarge at 125% to bring it up to full size.

Priscilla Hauser's Book of Fruit & Berries

MATERIALS

PAINT: Plaid FolkArt Acrylics
(A) = Artists' Pigments

Taffy

Hauser Green
Dark (A)

Hauser Green
Medium (A)

Hauser Green
Light (A)

Titanium White
(A)

Warm White (A)

Yellow Light (A)

MediumYellow (A)

Turner's Yellow (A)

Raw Sienna (A)

Burnt Sienna (A)

Pure Orange (A)

Red Light (A)

True Burgundy (A)

Burnt Umber (A)

Pure Black (A)

Dioxazine Purple
(A)

Prussian Blue (A)

Pure Magenta (A)

Yellow Citron (A)

Surface
• Wooden table (flea market find)

Brushes
• 1-inch (25mm) foam brush
• ¾-inch (19mm) wash brush
• Nos. 2, 4, 8, 12, 14 and 16 flats
• No. 3 round
• No. 1 liner

Additional Supplies
• General supplies from page 6
• Scissors
• Contact paper
• FolkArt Glazing Medium
• FolkArt Floating Medium
• FolkArt Blending Gel Medium
• See-through ruler

Prepare the Surface

1 Stain the table with glazing medium + Asphaltum and let dry. Measure in from the outer edges of the tabletop depending on how large you want your tiles; I have a 2-inch (51mm) border. Put tape on the outside edge of the line on all four sides.

2 You can choose to paint the entire tile area with Taffy, but then you have a sealed surface. If you want to make the blending easier you'll want to paint on an unsealed surface. First, transfer the outline of the design to the surface.

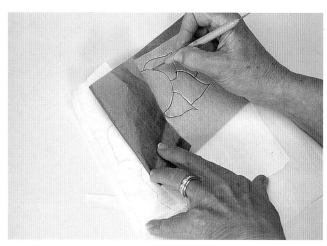

3 Trace the outer edge of the design on a piece of contact paper using graphite paper. Make sure you transfer the design on the top side of the contact paper.

4 Cut out the contact paper design.

5 Peel the contact paper away from the backing.

6 Place the contact paper carefully within the chalked outline on the surface. Press to seal all edges.

7 Paint the tile area with Taffy. Basecoat right on top of the contact paper. Keep the Taffy extremely thin so as not to build up an edge. Let this dry completely.

8 Carefully, remove the contact paper from the surface.

9 Draw your tiles on with a see-through ruler and a pencil. Keep your pencil lines light. I have created four tiles, but feel free to create more if you desire.

10 Use chalk to transfer the complete fruit design to the surface.

Prepare the Surface, CONTINUED

11 Double load a ¾-inch (19mm) flat brush with glazing medium and a little Raw Sienna. You don't want a lot of color. Softly blend on a sheet of tracing paper. This helps distribute the paint through the brush.

12 Float the color around the tile edges. Work on one tile at a time. Let this dry.

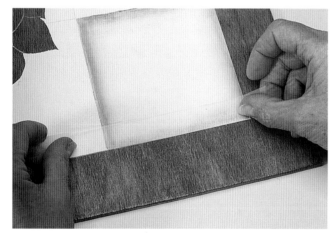

13 Place a fresh piece of tape over the outer edge of your tiles, buffing down the edges of the tape with your fingernail.

14 Paint the border with Hauser Green Dark using a sponge brush. Let this dry and carefully remove the tape.

15 In all four corners of the tiles put three comma strokes and a dot as shown. Use a no. 3 round brush loaded with a thin mix of Raw Sienna + Hauser Green Light.

16 Paint the grout using a no. 1 liner brush loaded with thin Burnt Umber. This will help separate the tiles.

The Border

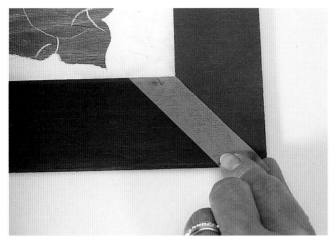

17 Tape the corner diagonally to create the mitered corners.

18 Mix 1 part Pure Black + 4 parts glazing medium and brush it lightly on the border.

19 Wipe some of the excess off with a paper towel leaving a dark stain.

20 Using a no. 1 liner brush loaded with Pure Black thinned with water, paint a line diagonally in the corners to create the miter.

The Fruit

APPLE STEP BY STEP

1 Carefully apply blending gel. The colors are applied below the point of dimension, where the stem comes down and joins the apple.

2 Using a light touch and a large brush, blend follwing the curve of the apple.

3 Apply a heavy yellow smile above the blended area and a hat on top of the smile.

4 Pull the yellow smile down into the apple. Be sure your strokes curve with the shape of the apple. Use plenty of paint.

5 Behind the yellow I added a little more red.

6 Add a smile of True Burgundy and pull ths smile down into the apple. Be sure when you pull, that the corners of the smile are rounded. Add a touch of Prussain Blue where the stem joins the apple.

PEAR STEP BY STEP

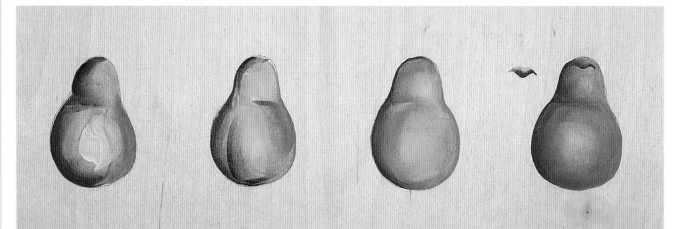

1 Apply the desired colors to the pear. Colors may vary as you wish. Wipe the brush.

2 Blend following the pear's natural curve. Be sure to create the triangle shape where the upper portion joins the lower portion of the pear.

3 Add more blending gel medium and paint if needed.

4 The point of dimension is achieved by double loading the brush with glazing medium and Burnt Sienna. Glaze the pear, if you wish, with Burnt Sienna or Red Light.

BERRIES STEP BY STEP

1 Apply Yellow Citron, Pure Magenta, Dioxazine Purple and Prussian Blue. The bracts are undercoated with Hauser Green Light.

2 Shade the bracts with a mixture of Hauser Green Dark + a touch of Prussian Blue and blend gently. Apply more blending gel.

3 Use a tiny flat brush side loaded with Titanium White to paint ¾-inch (19 mm) circles all the way around the outside edge and staggered working in toward the center.

4 To finish, add a complete circle or two in the center area of the berry, highlight each little section with a dot of white.

PLUM STEP BY STEP

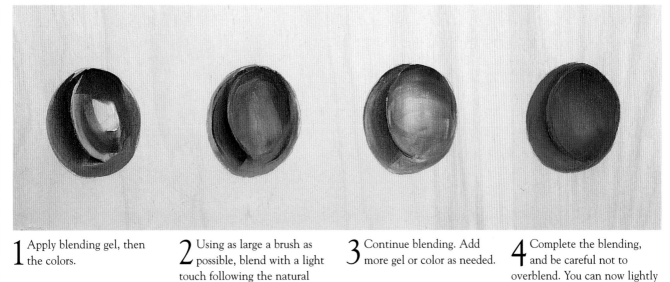

1 Apply blending gel, then the colors.

2 Using as large a brush as possible, blend with a light touch following the natural curve of the plum.

3 Continue blending. Add more gel or color as needed.

4 Complete the blending, and be careful not to overblend. You can now lightly mop away your brushstrokes.

The Final Touches

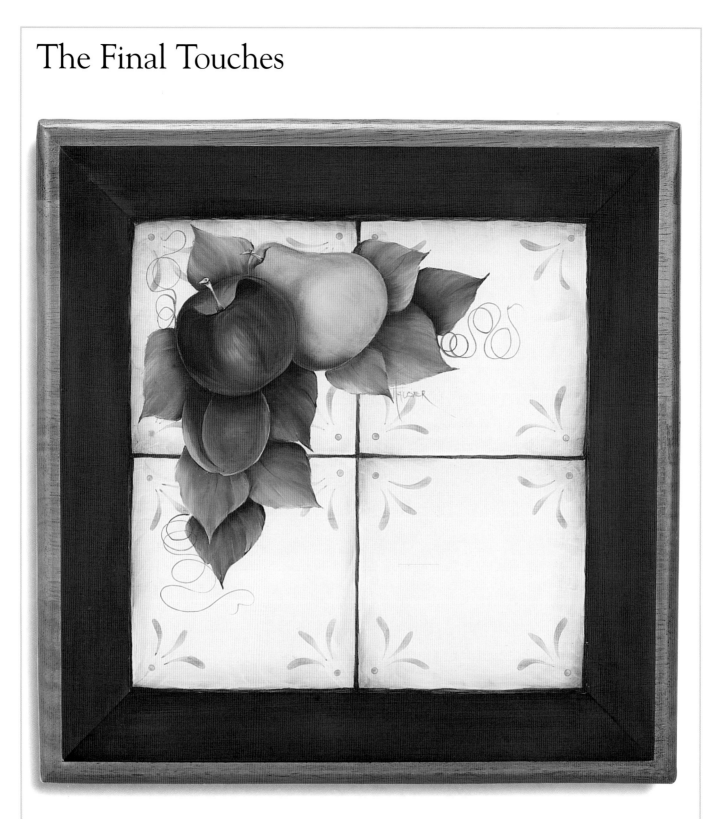

The Completed Table Top

The Completed Table

Fruit Garland on Faux Tile Table

A Tisket, a Tasket Apples on a Basket

9

A tisket, a tasket, let's paint green and yellow apples on a basket. Red apples have always been my favorite, but the green and yellow apples are beautiful too. There's a little less contrast in them, so they'll take a little more concentration when you paint them. Remember it is always easier to paint on an unsealed surface when blending than on a sealed surface. This is because the wood stays wet longer making those fast-drying acrylics work longer. I hope you'll enjoy this wonderful apple lesson.

This pattern may be hand-traced or photo-copied for personal use only. Enlarge at 182% to bring it up to full size.

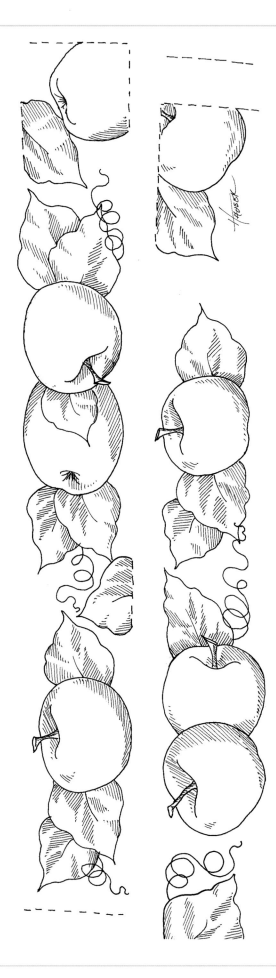

MATERIALS

PAINT: Plaid FolkArt Acrylics
(A) = Artists' Pigments

Hauser Green
Dark (A)

Hauser Green
Medium (A)

Hauser Green
Light (A)

Green Umber (A)

Burnt Umber (A)

Ice Blue (A)

Warm White (A)

Titanium White
(A)

Yellow Light (A)

Medium Yellow
(A)

Turner's Yellow (A)

Yellow Ochre (A)

Burnt Sienna (A)

Surface
- Wooden basket (flea market find)

Brushes
- ¾-inch (19mm) mop
- Nos. 4, 8, 10, 12, 14 and 16 flats
- No. 1 liner

Additional Supplies
- General supplies from page 6
- FolkArt Blending Gel Medium
- FolkArt Floating Medium
- FolkArt Glazing Medium

The Yellow Apple

PAINTING ON AN UNSEALED SURFACE

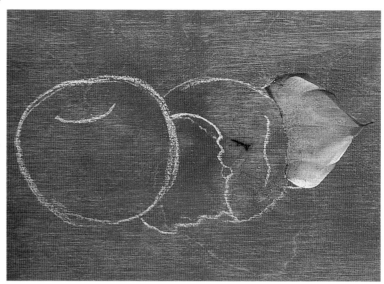

1 Apply blending gel to the leaf.

2 Paint the leaf as instructed on pages 15-17.

3 Begin the yellow apple by applying blending gel to the area. Using a no. 12 flat brush, start with white in the center, then apply Yellow Light around that. Apply Medium Yellow around the Yellow Light. Wipe the brush in between colors. Double load the brush with the two yellows and stroke above the center and next to the leaf. Load Hauser Green Light on the dirty brush and stroke along the top edge. Finally, load the dirty brush with Burnt Sienna and apply to the lower edge for shading.

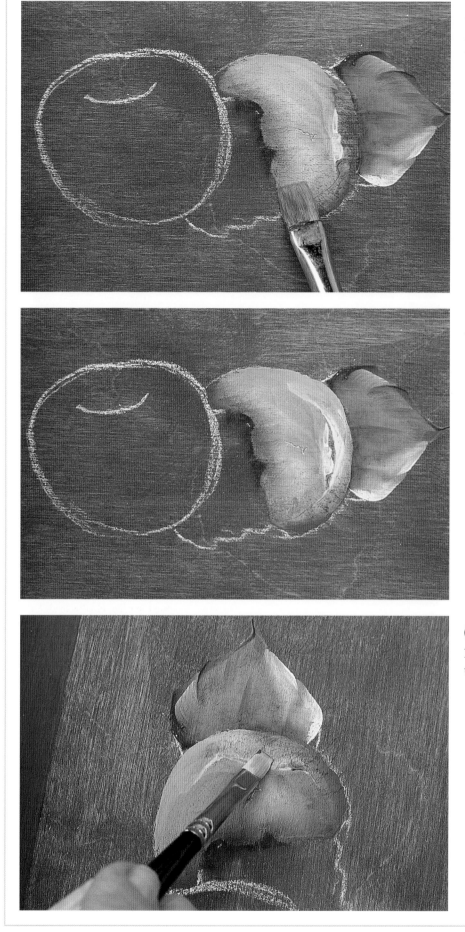

4 Blend the colors following the contours of the apple. Add more color if you would like to. I added a little Hauser Green Light.

5 Add a Yellow Light hat to the blossom end.

6 Apply Burnt Sienna above the hat on the dark side. Apply Hauser Green Light above the hat on the light side. Pull the Burnt Sienna down into the hat.

The Yellow Apple, CONTINUED

7 Lightly pull the Yellow Light into the Burnt Sienna, and into the Hauser Green Light.

8 Add a smile of Burnt Sienna for depth. Lightly pull the Burnt Sienna down into the left apple.

NOTE

If the lower part of the apple is not wet, add more blending gel medium and more paint. Then, pull down the Burnt Sienna smile.

9 Fill a no. 1 liner with Burnt Sienna thinned with water. Paint tiny umber dabs to create the blossom end.

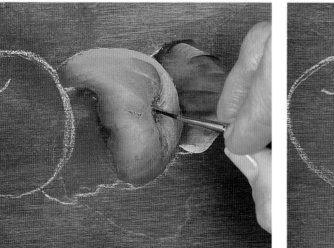

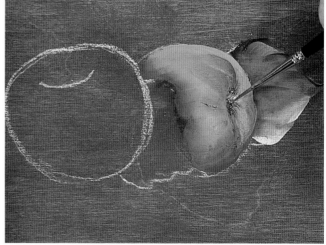

10 Pull a few lines out from the dots you just created.

11 Scatter a few thin Titanium White dots on the blossom end to create highlights.

The Green Apple

PAINTING ON A SEALED SURFACE

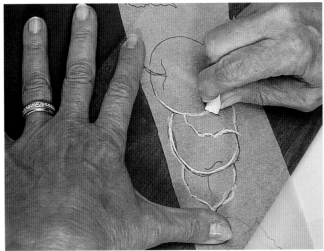

1 Basecoat the sides of the basket with Hauser Green Dark. Let dry and cure. Prepare the pattern for transfer by applying chalk to the backside of the pattern.

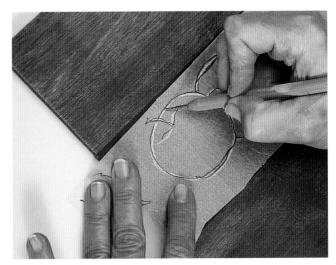

2 Transfer your pattern to the basecoated surface.

3 Undercoat the green apples with Hauser Green Light and the yellow apples with Medium Yellow using a no. 10 flat brush. Undercoat the leaves with a no. 8 flat brush loaded with Hauser Green Light. You'll need to apply two coats of each color to cover the basecoat. Let this dry and cure.

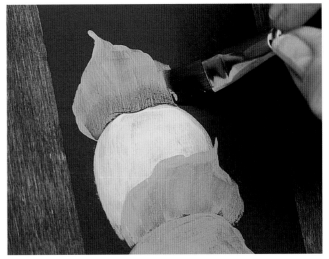

4 Anchor the shadows with a no. 14 flat brush side loaded with Green Umber and floating medium. Float the shadow on the leaves.

NOTE

Use as large a brush as possible when floating color.

The Green Apple, CONTINUED

5 The detailed instructions for painting the yellow apple and leaves are on pages 118-120.

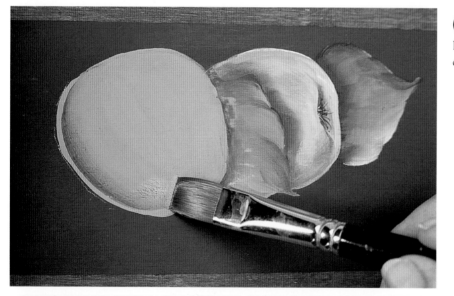

6 Anchor the shadows on the green apple using a no. 14 flat brush side loaded with Hauser Green Dark. Let this dry and cure.

7 Apply enough blending gel so the brush skates across the surface.

8 With a no. 10 flat brush, place Titanium White in the center, then Yellow Light around that. Apply Hauser Green Medium around the Yellow Light. Load the dirty brush with Hauser Green Light and apply along the right side. Wipe the brush between colors, but do not clean the brush. Water is not our friend when using blending techniques. For shading, load the dirty brush with Hauser Green Dark and apply along the left side.

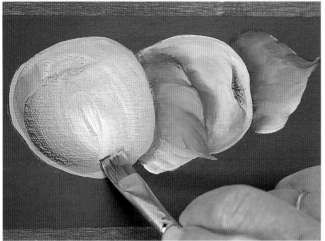

9 Blend the colors vertically. Always follow the contour of the apple.

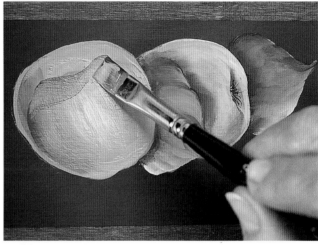

10 Put a smile on the apple using the wiped brush and Hauser Green Dark.

11 Lightly pull the smile down following the curve of the apple.

The Green Apple, CONTINUED

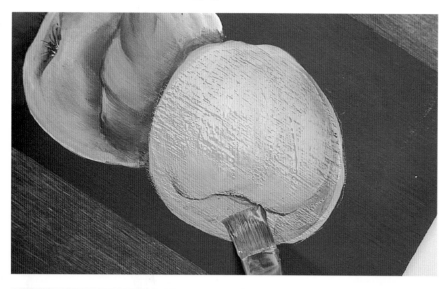

12 Apply a hat of Hauser Green Medium. Apply Hauser Green Dark above the hat on the dark side and Hauser Green Light above the hat on the light side.

13 Pull the Hauser Green Dark down into the hat.

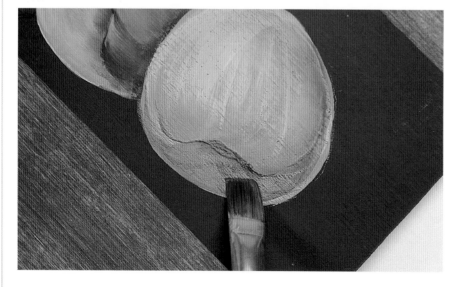

14 Pull the Hauser Green Dark up into the lighter green. Remember, you can turn your work to make painting easier.

15 Coordinate all the colors in the design by glazing the leaves and apples. Apply a little water or glazing medium to the leaves or apples, working one at a time.

16 If needed, glaze a little Hauser Green Dark over the leaves using a no. 14 flat brush.

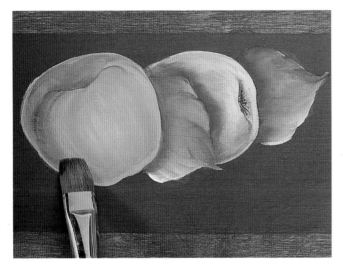

17 Glaze the green apple with Medium Yellow using the no. 14 flat brush. Let dry. Then, glaze with Burnt Sienna using the no. 14 flat brush.

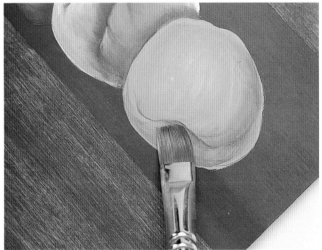

18 Add a little Burnt Sienna in the stem area as well.

19 Paint the stem as instructed on page 126.

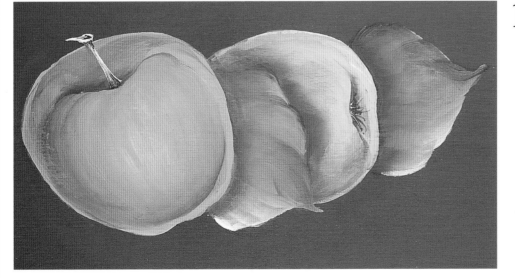

The Final Touches

STEM STEP BY STEP

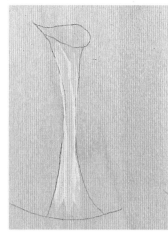 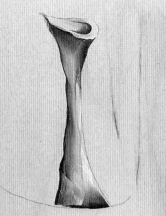 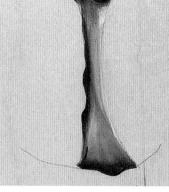

1 Apply blending gel. Then apply Titanium White.

2 Double load with Titanium White and Burnt Umber. Apply the shading and the U-stroke in the cut end.

3 Continue blending with a light touch. You may add more dark or light as needed.

4 Finish blending.

As you can see painted on a sealed or unsealed surface will give you the same results, but you need to understand how your paints will perform on both surfaces. It is my opinion that it is easier to blend on an unsealed surface.